The Silence of the Lamberts

**Other Close to Home Books
by John McPherson**

Close to Home
One Step Closer to Home
Dangerously Close to Home
Home: The Final Frontier
The Honeymoon Is Over

Treasury Collection

Close to Home Revisited

Also from John McPherson

High School Isn't Pretty
Close to Home: A Book of Postcards

The Silence of the Lamberts

A CLOSE TO HOME
COLLECTION
BY JOHN McPHERSON

Andrews and McMeel
A Universal Press Syndicate Company
Kansas City

──────────── ATTENTION: SCHOOLS AND BUSINESSES ────────────

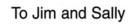

To Jim and Sally

"Our idiot veterinarian said that the cat has a serious tartar problem and recommended that I try flossing her teeth!"

" . . . and this is Miney, and this is Mo."

"OK, fine! If that's the way you wanna play, *I'll* make obnoxious gurgling sounds the next time *you're* putting for birdie!"

"That's nothin'! *I've* got a friend who was in labor for sixty-seven hours, she couldn't take any medication because she's allergic, and in the midst of it all the entire maternity staff went on strike and her baby had to be delivered by a janitor."

"OK, listen *very* carefully. Take this pill. If you start to feel numbness in your legs or have trouble pronouncing vowels, pull it out immediately."

By tapping into the stabilizing power
of gyroscopes, Wade was able to teach
his son to walk at just five months.

A new service for people who call in sick
and spend the day playing in the sun.

"They're *perfect*, Charles! I'll think of you
every time I wear them."

"Well, sure, honey, I'll take another cup of your tea.
That's very sweet of you."

Nobody was too pleased with the
yearbook staff at Whatney High.

"We apologize if we startled you, folks. However,
state law requires that we perform unannounced
Heimlich maneuver drills once every month."

"I can't believe I locked myself out again. Thank heavens for these clever hide-a-keys!"

"The plumber said he ran into some unexpected problems and will be back sometime next week."

As the last item was being rung up, Alan realized he had shopped with a list that had been lying in the cart, not the one his wife had given him.

Larry Vulmer: the Comb-Over King.

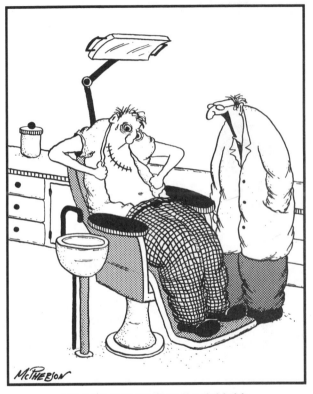

"That wisdom tooth on the right side
was giving me a tough time. So I had to
get at it from a different angle."

As someone who can never remember names,
Roger relied on his new Insta-Name to bail
him out of awkward social situations.

"Unfortunately, ma'am, this airplane is not equipped
with rest rooms. We do, however, have this personal
lavatory and a privacy blanket for your convenience."

"It certainly is an enthusiastic staff."

Hugh tries out his new Swiss Army Golf Clubs.

TV viewing changes forever with the
innovation of Surround-TV.

TLS Industries had a tendency to overmanage its employees.

To help customers fit into the bathing suits they wanted, Felman's Department Store wisely installed stair-stepping machines in its women's department.

Although no one at the table had said a word about it, Doug and Sandy sensed that they were being fixed up.

Ray hoped that the stroller would put an end to strangers referring to Jason as a "cute little girl."

"If they come after you, try to run this direction so I can get it on video."

Darren decides to get the roll-bar option
on his in-line skates.

"*Independence Day* wasn't available, but I found
something I think you'll like even better.
It's a Lithuanian film with Tibetan subtitles."

Bob was starting to sense that someone in management had it in for him.

"Jerry, the claims adjuster is here."

" . . . with anchovies, mushrooms and extra cheese.
Deliver it to 157 Pinehurst. If we're not here, take it
to the maternity wing of Glenview Hospital."

"Dr. Bickford is trying out a new inoculation method
he found out about when he was traveling in Borneo."

Auto-repair shops continue to become
more specialized.

Every once in a while, just for kicks, Dr. Fernlock liked to
amplify his drill through the office's stereo system.

"And how about you, ma'am? Would you like
some ground pepper on your salad?"

" . . . and one bottle of extra-potent calcium supplements!"

With quality child care becoming tougher to find, many couples are incorporating day-care enrollment into their wedding ceremony.

"This new choir director certainly has spunk."

Karl takes the concept of vanity plates to previously unknown levels of narcissism.

Another gullible parent is sucked in by
pharmaceutical quackery.

The Litmans' discovery of the tunnel alerted them
to an alarming fact: Tippy was leading a double
life as someone else's pet.

Hoover introduces its new vacuum cleaner bags, which, when full, become collectible celebrity replicas.

Thanks to her new personal toddler fence, Janet no longer had to worry about losing track of her kids in crowds.

With final exams in full swing, the administration
brought out the cheat-sheet-sniffing dogs.

"I hate this hole."

Knowing that wedding receiving lines are notorious for being dull,
Pete and Gloria did their best to liven theirs up.

"Unfortunately, Carolyn, your
body has rejected your face lift."

To help him cope with what was certain to be
a tension-filled meeting, Dwight wore his new
battery-operated massage shirt.

State troopers along this stretch of I-90 were
known for their cunning at catching speeders.

Chairmaster: for those who want to ease
their way into the fitness scene.

How the IRS really decides whose
return gets audited.

"That new kid at the pizza shop is
starting to get on my nerves."

"I've seen unusual rashes before, but this is incredible! There's Fiji, and New Guinea! Look! You can even see snow on top of Mount Everest!"

"Ray? It's Vern. The computers are down again."

"I know every man needs to have a hobby,
but this is really starting to grate on me."

The pressure of the SAT finally pushes
Brian Folbert over the edge.

Many top-of-the-line fitness machines now come equipped with a motivational alarm that sounds if the machine is not used for at least twenty minutes a day.

Late in the day, when all of the popular videos have been rented, they appear: video scavengers who prey on customers returning videos.

50

A hideous new fad: 3-D tattoos.

Another case of carpool abuse.

Tensions mounted in the office as a gang of
IBM users strayed into the Mac users' turf.

"If you start to feel dizzy or weak, get outside
immediately. Your new pacemaker is solar-powered."

"Are you nuts?! Who in his right mind tries out a
jet ski in a backyard swimming pool?!!"

Every graduate's deepest fear.

"Hal and I used to get devoured by mosquitoes, but since we started wearing the bat houses, we haven't had a single bite."

"I jerked the wheel hard to the left to avoid hitting the squirrel,
and then I heard this horrible twisting noise."

"Personally, I think it's cruel to make the poor
things walk all that way through the tube,
but Gene likes to see them up close."

56

"We've made some revisions in our retirement program. In lieu of a pension, you'll now get one limited-edition Elvis collector's plate per pay period."

Constantly looking for enticing ways to
improve its menu, a major pizza chain
introduces its new pizza ball.

"It was George's last request, so I went through
with it. But it's making it real tough to find a
buyer for the house."

Overzealous parents continue to be a problem at
Little League parks throughout the country.

To help provide even speedier service to their customers, many fast-food restaurants have begun to employ psychics.

"For heaven's sake, Ray! Take a look at this!
That mousetrap you set last night has a little
doll caught in it that looks just like you!"

"If you get an itch, just turn whichever one
of these cranks is closest to it."

"Tom built a dollhouse for the girls with a full basement."

Fortunately, Chad was able to intercept his report card just as it was about to fall into the wrong hands.

Nick hoped that the new scope on his driver
would put an end to his horrendous slice.

An emerging service industry: wedding truancy officers.

"Hey, listen to this! According to the scorecard, this golf
course was designed by Stephen King!"

"I heard a loud clunking noise and then I ran over something large."

"There! I heard it again! There's a mosquito buzzing around here somewhere and *every time* I sit up, it stops!"

Most employees found that playing the new game in the cafeteria was a great way to relieve stress.

"That suit is called 'The Optical Illusion.'"

The Second Law of Grocery Shopping: If you shop for just a few items using one of the shopping baskets, you will inevitably find thirty or forty other items you need.

Warren makes a last-ditch effort to start his mower.

"If you don't mind, Mr. Morris, I'd like to get one more photo with you, me, and some of the ambulance attendants, and then we'll get you right over to X-ray."

The humiliating moment when you realize that the church program said to sing verses one, two, and three, but not four.

"We ran out of IV bags."

"For heaven's sake! We better use the SPF 45 today!"

"I just clocked you doin' 127 miles an hour!
You've got some explainin' to do, mister!"

Although the other employees adored him,
Wayne the stockboy had a dark side.

Before going out on a blind date, Claudia always checks out the guy thoroughly with her Weirdometer.

"Folks, we're going to give an old tradition a new twist. Rather than throw the bride's bouquet, we're going to open the gate and see which one of you lucky single gals can snatch the bouquet from old Cyclone here!"

"There you go, sir."

"The salesman said that these provide three times
the traction of regular golf shoes!"

"Let me see the cruise brochure again!"

At The National Academy of Mall Security Guards

"Us? We're fine! Bill had surgery on his lower back last month, but other than that, life's been pretty uneventful."

"Oh, that? That's my new automatic lawn-mowing system.
Step over here and I'll show you how it works."

"All right, Mrs. Clandell. Cover Muffin's right eye."

"Please put down the photo of
Cindy Crawford, ma'am."

**Due to recent cutbacks, several major airlines
have eliminated their snack carts.**

For those difficult bedtimes, Sheryl
relied on the bedtime reel.

One of life's unfailing truths: Whenever you pose for a group photo, the others will inevitably choose the photo in which you happen to look like a complete doofus.

"A Barbie doll got stuck under the brake pedal."

"Here you go! T-bone steak, mashed potatoes, and fresh asparagus! Whoops! What am I doing? This is for Mr. Cagner in room 173."

"Check and see if the stinger is still in me!"

"OK, now, Mr. Weston. Let's start by taking care of that tartar build-up."

89

"Yep, it's beavers, all right. That explains the missing legs to your coffee table."

"I'm starting to think that our early retirement program was a little *too* popular."

"Unfortunately, ma'am, our fitting rooms are being renovated. But if you'll just step behind this clothing rack, Betty and Rowena will be happy to stand guard for you while you change."

92

"I'm sorry, sir, but there's a four dollar
fee for asking questions."

"Calm down, Lois! You're getting all
worked up over nothing! Look at the shape
of its head! That snake's not poisonous!"

Yet another holiday is created by the gift industry.

What police officers are actually doing for all
that time when they've got you pulled over.

A sense of apathy was beginning to creep into the company's employee-of-the-month program.

The Thackleys couldn't help but be jealous of the Furmans' new all-terrain stroller.

"Don finally figured out a way to keep the squirrels from getting at the bird feeder."

"Mrs. Nortman just sent in this fax of a rash that she's got on her stomach."

97

The latest innovation in air travel: convertible jets.

Raymond tries out his new sweat-diverting eaves trough.

"Where the heck did you get this lava lamp, anyway?!"

"So much for our security deposit."

To discourage himself from using his credit card, Ray
got into the habit of duct-taping it to his stomach.

"Those are 100 percent turkey feathers! They never need painting, have ten times the R-value of vinyl siding, and not a single tree had to be cut down!"

"He says he's thirsty."

The Nilburns stumble onto the Secret
Toddler Treasure Trove.

With 150 miles to go and fatigue setting in, Alan
wisely turned on his anti-drowsiness device.

"Remind me never to play this course again."

Charlene took the business of screening
prospective roommates very seriously.

"It's a deodorant holder! This way you can put
deodorant on both underarms at the same time!"

Ultra-sensitive car alarms.

"I videotaped my jogging route so that on rainy days all I need to do is start the tape and run on the treadmill until I see our driveway."

"This way, if I wipe out, I'll roll instead of getting scuffed up."

"That's it, Wade! You've got him! Tighten up on the line a bit! Perfect! You're wearin' him down! . . ."

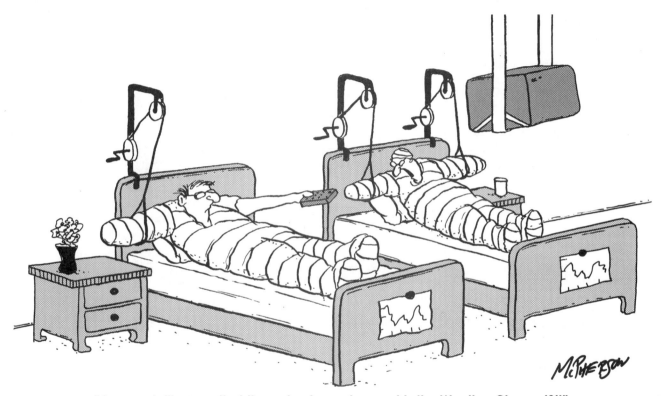

"Are you telling me that the only channel we get is the Weather Channel?!!"

THE NATIONAL DAY CARE HALL OF FAME

RYAN BELL
- POTTY TRAINED BY AGE 11 MONTHS
- AVG. NAP TIME, 4½ HRS.

TANYA ZEFF
- GOT DRESSED AND INTO CAR SEAT WITHOUT HELP BY AGE 11 MONTHS

ELLEN HOLT
- STARTED SLEEPING THROUGH THE NIGHT AT AGE 6 DAYS

REGGIE NURBIT
- NEVER CRIED, EVEN WHEN MARBLE GOT STUCK IN NOSE ONE TIME.
- NEVER GOT SICK ONCE.

THE LUXLEY TWINS
- CHANGED EACH OTHER'S DIAPERS BY AGE 13 MONTHS.

AMY KEPPLE
PREPARED OWN FORMULA AT AGE 5 MONTHS

McPHERSON

"Bernice? Glenda Pratner up in 27-B. Hey, take a look out your dining room window and see if my air conditioner is hanging nearby and try to haul it inside."

"We're in luck, Dave! I found my Triple-A card!"

"Wait a second, Don! It's not broken! My knee had just loosened the plug! See?! It's working fine now!"

"Is this National Farm Insurance? I need $200,000 of tornado insurance! Make it effective right now! Here's my credit card number!"

Virgil's new Sippy-Cup Body Straw was the perfect way to cool off on a hot day.

"These kill seven times as many bugs per hour as bug zappers
and use only a third the electricity."

"We'd like to ask that the couple sitting behind us be
cut off from receiving any more cocktails."

"For heaven's sake, Frank, this is no time
to be a hero! Give them what they want!
You've got a family to think about!"

"This one's got a stopwatch, lap counter,
and is waterproof to a depth of 100 feet."

Unfortunately, Arnie's trick with the bubble gum did little to impress his interviewer.

"We had child safety gates built into the house. The collar Jason is wearing activates the gate anytime he gets within ten feet of the stairs."

"The doctor says the pin can come
out in three months."

"The video is due back at 7 p.m. tomorrow.
After that it will begin to emit a hideous stench.
Enjoy the movie!"

"Ed wanted to make sure that he'd have lots of visitors here, plus it provides a nice supplemental income for the family."

"We had it installed so we could get a fifteen percent reduction in our fire insurance premium, but we're starting to have a real problem with the dog."

"Unfortunately, ma'am, the fire department can't get here for another two hours. However, a gentleman at the top has volunteered to slide down and try to knock you free."

121

"According to the instructions, we can't drive faster than
three miles per hour or have a total passenger weight
over 150 pounds while the spare is being used."

"The in-flight movie is four dollars. If you're not
interested in the movie, we ask that you wear
one of these masks until the film is over."

"Look, I don't have a cent in the car. Here are four Chiclets and a ticket to my son's high school play."

"They're all out of those paper cones for the cotton candy."

To help boost the morale of employees in windowless offices, Voltech Industries installed TV monitors displaying live footage of a nearby window.

It dawned on Carol that today was the day the realtor had said he wanted to show the house.

"Unfortunately, Mrs. Dortford, our entire X-ray department is on strike. But if you'll just describe your pain in as much detail as possible, our staff sketch artist should be able to give us a fairly accurate drawing of the problem." 127

"I need everything except this for a '92 Ford Taurus."

"Nuts! I think we're going to need an adapter for this."

"Okee-doke! Let's just double-check. We're 130 feet up and we've got 45 yards of bungee cord, that's uh . . . 90 feet. Allow for 30 feet of stretching, that gives us a total of . . . 120 feet. Perfect!"